The Best Cat in the World

For Hayden,
Best wishes,

Lesléa Newman

For Marilyn and Shanti, with love
—*L. N.*

Text © 2004 by Lesléa Newman
Illustrations © 2004 by Ronald Himler
Published 2006 by Eerdmans Books for Young Readers
An imprint of Wm. B. Eerdmans Publishing Company
255 Jefferson S.E., Grand Rapids, Michigan 49503
P.O. Box 163, Cambridge CB3 9PU U.K.

06 07 08 09 10 11 8 7 6 5

Library of Congress Cataloging-in-Publication Data
Newman, Lesléa.
The best cat in the world / written by Lesléa Newman ; [illustrated by Ronald Himler].
p. cm.

ISBN-10: 0-8028-5252-1 / ISBN-13: 978-0-8028-5252-6 (hardcover : alk. paper)
ISBN-10: 0-8028-5294-7 / ISBN-13: 978-0-8028-5294-6 (paper : alk. paper)

Summary: A young boy deals with the loss of his beloved cat, Charlie,
eventually accepting the arrival of another, very different cat.
[1. Cats-Fiction. 2. Grief-Fiction.] I. Himler, Ronald, ill. II.
Title.
PZ7.N47988Be 2004
[E]--dc22
2003013028

The illustrations were created with watercolor and pencil on paper.
The type was set in New Baskerville.
Graphic Designer Matthew Van Zomeren

The Best Cat in the World

Written by Lesléa Newman   Illustrated by Ronald Himler

Eerdmans Books for Young Readers
Grand Rapids, Michigan • Cambridge, U.K.

When Sam was a kitten, he had orange fur the color of a Halloween pumpkin and big green eyes that looked like two lucky marbles to keep in your pocket. But now Sam was old. His orange fur was full of white patches, and grey clouds floated across his eyes. Sam used to play with his favorite toy, a ball of red yarn tied to a stick, all the time. But now Sam was too tired to play. Mostly he just napped on my bed. At night he slept on a special pillow right next to mine. "Who's the best cat in the world?" I asked him after Mom turned off the light. Sam purred a rumbling reply.

One day Sam he didn't get up at all, not even for his supper. We took him to the vet, but there was nothing she could do. "I can't make Sam young again," Dr. Levin said as she stroked Sam s head. "I'm sorry, Victor." A few days later, Sam died.

I cried and cried for two whole days. Mom didn't even make me go to school. We buried Sam in the backyard and planted a rosebush for him with green leaves and orange flowers.

Everyone was nice to me when Sam he died. Sam s vet sent me a special card with a picture of an orange cat on it. Mom made my favorite supper, macaroni and cheese, three nights in a row, but every time I tried to eat it, I just cried. My teacher put a picture of Sam up on the bulletin board at school and all the kids drew pictures of him. But I was still sad.

I sat in front of Sam 's rosebush after school and tried to talk to him. "Who's the best cat in the world?" I asked. Then I listened as hard as I could, but there was no reply.

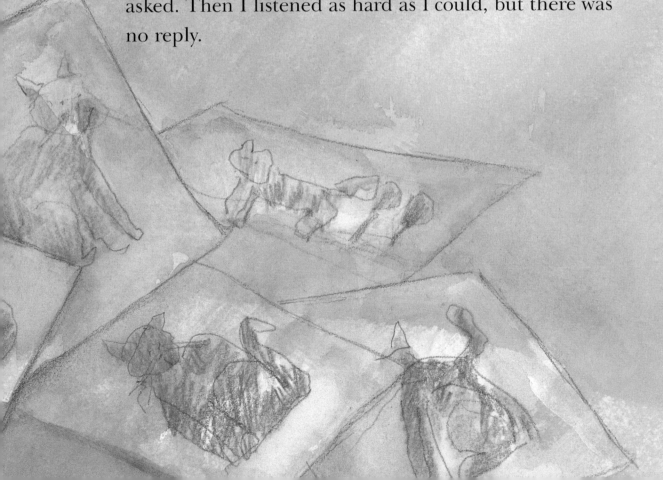

One day Mom came outside and sat down next to me by Sam rosebush. "You miss Sam a lot, don't you, Victor?" she asked. My words got all stuck in my throat so I just nodded.

"Maybe it's time for us to get a new cat," Mom
said softly.

"Sam's rosebush grew all blurry. "I don't want a new
cat," I said, wiping my wet cheeks. "I want Sam."

A few weeks later, Dr. Levin called. "Victor, I have a big problem," she said. "Someone brought me a brand-new kitten, and I need to find a very special home for her right away," she said. "Do you know anyone who loves cats?"

"I love cats."

"Perfect," Dr. Levin said. "Would you like to come meet this kitty?"

"I don't know," I said to Mom. "Maybe Sam would get mad if we brought another cat here."

"Maybe," Mom said. "Or, maybe he'd be happy that we were giving another cat such a good home."

"But what if I don't like her?" I asked, putting on my jacket. "Or maybe she won't like me."

"Let's meet her first, before you make up your mind." Mom picked up her car keys, and we went out the door.

When we got to Dr. Levin's office, she showed us the kitten. Her fur was all different colors—brown and grey and red and black and white—and her eyes were the color of two perfectly toasted marshmallows, a beautiful golden brown.

"She's a tortoiseshell kitten, so we've named her Phobe," Dr. Levin said, handing her to me.

"Hi, Phobe," I said. I tried to drape her over my back the way I used to hold Charlie, but Phobe didn't like that. She snuggled into my neck and licked my chin.

"I think Phobey wants to come home with us," Mom said, and Dr. Levin agreed. "What do you think, Victor?"

I held Phobe up to get a better look at her, and she tapped her paw against my cheek. "Yes," I said. "I think so, too."

When we got home, I gave Phoebey some food in a
brand-new bowl and knelt down to scratch her between
the ears while she ate. She hissed and ducked her
head away.

"Some cats don't like to be touched when they eat,"
Mom said.

"Sam did," I reminded her.

"I know," Mom said. "But that's not Sam."

After Shelley ate I tried to play with her, but she wanted to take a nap. She slept on the couch in the living room instead of on my bed like Charlie always did.

At suppertime, Charlie always sat under my chair and waited for me to drop him table scraps when Mom wasn't looking. "Pssst, Shelley," I whispered, when Mom got up to get a spoon. "Here's a piece of chicken."

But Shelley didn't want to sit under my chair, and she wasn't interested in chicken. She curled up by the stove where it was nice and warm and cleaned herself all the way down to the tip of her tail.

At bedtime, I put Shelley on a special pillow right next to mine, but she jumped down even before Mom turned out the light and leaped up onto my windowsill where she slept all night long.

The next morning, I didn't wake up until seven-thirty. Charlie used to wake me up every day at exactly ten after seven by poking his cold, wet nose into my hand. Mom used to say you could set your clock by Charlie. I went over to the windowsill where Shelley was still sleeping.

"You're supposed to wake me up," I told her, but she just yawned and stretched her paws.

When I went into the bathroom to brush my teeth,
Shelley leaped up on the sink and tried to catch drops
of water from the faucet with her tongue. Charlie
never did that.

When I got dressed, Shelley grabbed my shoelaces
with her paw and tried to bite them. Charlie never
did that either.

Before I left for school, I picked Shelley up to say goodbye. She snuggled into my neck and licked my chin, just like she did at the vet's office.

When I got home from school, Shelley was sleeping on the couch. I started to pet her, and she rolled over so I could rub her belly. It was soft and warm. Charlie never let me touch his belly.

I went into the kitchen for a snack, and then I got out
Charlie's favorite toy to see if Shelley wanted to play
with it. I twirled the yarn in the air, and Shelley jumped
up and caught it just like Charlie used to. But she didn't
pull it away with her head held high and the stick
dragging behind her like Charlie always did. Shelley
rolled onto her back, held it with all four paws, and
started chewing it. I wonder why Charlie never thought
of that.

At suppertime, Shelley sat in the middle of the kitchen and watched us eat. Then she started chasing her tail. She ran round and round in circles, and Mom and I laughed.

"Charlie never chased his tail," Mom said.

"I know," I said. "But that's not Charlie."

When it was time for bed, Shelley jumped up on my windowsill. There were lots of stars in the sky and the moon was shining on Charlie's rosebush.

"Who's the best cat in the world?" I asked Shelley. She looked at me, blinked her eyes twice, and purred a rumbling reply.